Readers' Theater: How to Put on a Production
Groundhogs and Guinea Pigs

A Readers' Theater Script and Guide

Looking Glass Library

An Imprint of Magic Wagon
abdopublishing.com

By Nancy K. Wallace   Illustrated by Nina Mata

To Lucy and Olivia, who don't like storms. —NKW
To my parents, my loving husband Aaron & my darling Aria. —NM

abdopublishing.com

Published by Magic Wagon, a division of ABDO, PO Box 398166, Minneapolis, Minnesota 55439.
Copyright © 2016 by Abdo Consulting Group, Inc. International copyrights reserved in all countries. No part
of this book may be reproduced in any form without written permission from the publisher. Looking Glass Library™
is a trademark and logo of Magic Wagon.

Printed in the United States of America, North Mankato, Minnesota.
042015
092015

THIS BOOK CONTAINS
RECYCLED MATERIALS

Written by Nancy K. Wallace
Illustrations by Nina Mata
Edited by Heidi M.D. Elston, Megan M. Gunderson & Bridget O'Brien
Designed by Laura Mitchell

Library of Congress Cataloging-in-Publication Data

Wallace, Nancy K.
  Groundhogs and guinea pigs : a readers' theater script and guide / by Nancy K. Wallace ; illustrated by Nina Mata.
     pages cm. -- (Readers' theater : how to put on a production set 2)
  ISBN 978-1-62402-114-5
1. Groundhog Day--Juvenile drama. 2. Children's plays, American. 3. Theater--Production and direction--Juvenile
literature. 4. Readers' theater--Juvenile literature. I. Mata, Nina, 1981- illustrator. II. Title.
  PS3623.A4436G76 2016
  812'.6--dc23
                    2015002816

Table of Contents

Celebrate with a Play!

Everyone loves holidays! Some schools and libraries hold programs or assemblies to commemorate special occasions. This series offers fun plays to help celebrate six different holidays at your school or library. You can even sell tickets and use your play as a fund-raiser.

Readers' theater can be done very simply. The performers sit on stools or chairs onstage. They don't have to memorize their lines. They just read them.

Adapted readers' theater looks more like a regular play. The stage includes scenery and props. The performers wear makeup and costumes. They move around to show the action. But, they still carry their scripts.

Readers' theater scripts can also be used for puppet shows. The performers stand behind a curtain, move the puppets, and read their scripts.

Find a place large enough to put on a play. An auditorium with a stage is ideal. A classroom will work, too. Choose a date and ask permission to use the space. Advertise your play with posters and flyers. Place them around your school and community. Tell your friends and family. Everyone enjoys watching a fun performance!

Tickets and Playbills

Tickets and playbills can be handwritten or designed on a computer. Be sure tickets include the title of the play. They should list the date, time, and location of the performance.

A playbill is a printed program. The front of a playbill has the title of the play, the date, and the time. The cast and crew are listed inside. Be sure to have enough playbills for the audience and cast. Pass them out at the door as the audience enters.

The Crew

Next, a crew is needed. The show can't go on without these important people! Some jobs can be combined for a small show.

Director — organizes everyone and everything in the show.

Costume Designer — designs and borrows or makes all the costumes.

Stage Manager — makes sure everything runs smoothly.

Lighting Designer — runs spotlights and other lighting.

Set Designer — plans and makes scenery.

Prop Manager — finds, makes, and keeps track of props.

Special Effects Crew — takes care of sound and other special effects.

Sets

At a readers' theater production, the performers can sit on stools at the front of the room. An adapted readers' theater production or full play will require sets and props. A set is the background that creates the setting for each scene. A prop is an item the actors use onstage.

Scene 1 and scene 2 take place in the library. You will need a table, two chairs, and a painted background of bookcases. If you use real bookcases, make sure they are easy to move onstage.

Scene 3 takes place outside the school. Use fiberfill to cover artificial trees with "snow."

Scene 4 and scene 5 take place in the classroom. Use desks or tables and chairs for the students. Make a window out of cardboard.

Props

- Stack of library books
- Large picture of a groundhog
- Black construction paper
- Glue sticks
- Book on groundhogs
- Calendar
- 3 fake snowballs
- Guinea pig cage
- Shoe box
- Carrots

Special Effects

Design a cardboard window for scene 4 and cut out the panes. Stage crew can gently throw snow outside the window for a realistic effect!

The Cast

Decide who will play each part. Each person in the cast will need a script. All of the performers should practice their lines. Reading lines aloud over and over will help the performers learn them. *Groundhogs and Guinea Pigs* needs the following cast:

Michael — a student in Mr. Pacella's class

Mr. Pacella — a third grade teacher

Jake — Michael's best friend

Miss Sharon — the school librarian

Tori — a student in Mr. Pacella's class

Class — students in Mr. Pacella's class

Makeup and Costumes

Makeup artists have a big job! Every cast member wears makeup. And, stage makeup needs to be brighter and heavier than regular makeup. Buy several basic shades of mascara, foundation, blush, and lipstick. Apply with a new cotton ball or swab for each cast member to avoid spreading germs.

Costume designers set the scene as much as set designers. They borrow costumes or adapt old clothing for each character. Ask adults for help finding and sewing costumes.

Most of the performers in this play can wear regular clothes they would wear to school. There are a few exceptions.

Michael, Tori, **Jake**, and their classmates should dress in regular school clothes. In scenes 3 and 5, the three friends should wear winter coats with hats, scarves, and mittens.

Mr. Pacella should wear a shirt and tie.

Miss Sharon can wear a dress or skirt.

Rehearsals and Stage Directions

After you decide to put on a play, it is important to set up a rehearsal schedule. Choose a time everyone can attend, such as after school or on weekends. Try to have at least five rehearsals before the performance.

Everyone should practice together as a team, even though individual actors will be reading their own scripts. This will help the play sound like a conversation, instead of separate lines. Onstage, actors should act like their characters even when they aren't speaking.

In the script, stage directions are in parentheses. They are given from the performer's point of view, not the audience's. Actors face the audience when performing, so left is on their left and right is on their right.

Some theater terms may be unfamiliar:

Curtains — the main curtain at the front of the stage.

House — the area in which the audience sits.

Wings — the part of the stage on either side that the audience can't see.

Right Wing
Stage Right

Upstage
Center Stage
Downstage

Left Wing
Stage Left

Script: Groundhogs and Guinea Pigs

Scene 1: The School Library

(Set the scene with two chairs as well as a table covered in books. Use a real bookshelf or paint some on cardboard. Michael and Tori sit facing the audience.)

Michael: Who's making the groundhog cookies?

Tori: My mom's baking sugar cookies. I'm helping her make chocolate frosting! We'll bring M&Ms for noses and chocolate chips for eyes. Everyone can decorate their own.

Michael: *(Closes his eyes and smiles.)* I *love* sugar cookies! I want three or four!

Tori: *(Laughing.)* She knows, Michael. She'll bring lots. What about the Pin the Top Hat on the Groundhog game?

Michael: *(Holding up a picture of a groundhog.)* I made the groundhog.

Tori: *(Clapping her hands.)* That's so cute! I love his face. You did a really good job.

Michael: Thanks! I still need to make the top hats.

Tori: *(Standing up.)* I can help with that. I'll go ask Mr. Pacella for some black construction paper. *(Exits stage right.)*

Michael: *(Shouting after her.)* Ask for glue sticks, too. We're out!

Jake: *(Enters stage left.)* Hey, nice deal! You and Tori got out of science class!

Michael: Only because we're helping plan the class Groundhog Day party!

Jake: That's such a weird idea for a party. Do you think Mr. Pacella will dress up like a groundhog?

Michael: No way! He's a shirt and tie guy.

Jake: Do they even make groundhog costumes?

Michael: They probably wouldn't sell very many. Groundhog Day only comes once a year.

Jake: So does Christmas and look how many Santa Claus costumes they sell.

Michael: True, but Santa brings gifts. Groundhogs just bring weather, and that's not very exciting.

Tori: *(Enters stage right.)* Groundhogs don't bring weather. They forecast it.

Jake: I bet they aren't very good at forecasting it, either.

Michael: They're probably never right!

Tori: Everyone is right some of the time. We're in the library. We can just look it up!

Scene 2: The School Library – a few minutes later

(Miss Sharon pretends to put books away. She turns around as Tori, Michael, and Jake enter from stage left.)

Tori: Miss Sharon, we want to find out if the Groundhog Day weather forecast is ever right.

Miss Sharon: *(Puts an armload of books on the table.)* I have a groundhog book right here, since the holiday is coming up. *(Turning the pages of the book.)* It looks like the groundhog's forecast is right only 39% of the time.

Michael: Well, that's not very good!

Jake: If I got 39% on a science test, I would fail.

Michael: *(Whispering.)* You *did* get 39% on a science test last month!

Jake: *(Whispering and laughing.)* Shh, don't tell!

Miss Sharon: Look at this. *(She holds up a calendar.)* Here's Groundhog Day on February 2. Here's the first day of spring this year, March 20th. How many weeks are there in between?

Michael: It's about six and a half weeks.

Miss Sharon: Usually the groundhog predicts six more weeks of winter.

Tori: But according to the calendar, we really *do* have six more weeks of winter!

Miss Sharon: Right! Officially, spring doesn't start until six weeks after Groundhog Day.

Tori: So why does everybody love Groundhog Day if it doesn't matter what he predicts?

Michael: Because it's fun!

Miss Sharon: You're absolutely right, Michael. Groundhog Day is fun! It comes right in the middle of winter when everyone needs a break. If he gives us good news about spring coming early, it makes everyone happy!

Jake: That's just weird!

Miss Sharon: Well, here's something even weirder. In Germany, they used hedgehogs to predict the weather! When German settlers came to Pennsylvania, they started using groundhogs instead because there weren't any hedgehogs.

Jake: How do they predict the weather? Animals can't talk.

Miss Sharon: By their behavior. If the groundhog sees his shadow when he comes out of his burrow in the morning on February 2, it means six more weeks of winter.

Jake: So, could you use any animal to predict the weather?

Miss Sharon: Well, it's supposed to be a hibernating animal.

Jake: What's that?

Miss Sharon: It's an animal that sleeps all winter long.

Tori: Like a bear!

Jake: Wow! I suddenly have a great idea for the party, guys. When can we talk about it?

Michael: *(Shrugging.)* After school, I guess.

Jake: See you then! *(Exits stage right.)*

(Tori and Michael turn to watch him go.)

Tori: What was that all about?

Michael: I have no idea.

Scene 3: Outside the School

(If there is a curtain, this scene can take place in front of it while the stage crew changes the scene to the classroom behind it. Or, this scene can take place in front of a backdrop of the school. Place a few small pine trees around the stage. Cover them with fiberfill, which will look like snow. Place white sheets or fabric around the bases of the trees to look like snowdrifts. Place two snowballs where Michael stands and give one to Jake.)

Tori: *(Stamping her feet as though she's cold.)* So, where is he?

Michael: You know Jake, he's always late. *(Bends down and pretends to make a snowball.)*

Tori: *(Folding her arms over her chest.)* Well, I'm freezing! If he doesn't come in two minutes, I'm going home.

Michael: There he is! *(Throwing a snowball off stage right.)*

Jake: *(Enters stage right carrying a snowball.)* Hey! No fair! I had to stay after class to talk to Mr. Pacella. I got a D on the science test on Monday.

Tori: Oh, Jake, I'm sorry. Do you need help studying?

Jake: No, it's okay. Mr. Pacella says I can do a special project to raise my grade.

Tori: Okay. Let us know if we can do anything.

Michael: So, what's your idea for the party? We're turning into icicles!

Jake: You know how Miss Sharon said you can use other animals to predict the weather?

Tori and **Michael:** *(Hesitantly.)* Yes …

Jake: Well, I got a new guinea pig a couple of months ago to be a roommate for Otto. His name is Gus.

Michael: *(Sounding unconvinced.)* Your guinea pig can't predict the weather, Jake!

Jake: Gus really can, Michael! Every time we're going to have a big storm, he curls up in his shoe box. He doesn't come out until it's over.

Michael: He's probably just sleepy.

Tori: Maybe not. I think animals can sense things. My dog always hides under my bed before a thunderstorm.

Michael: *(Making another snowball and throwing it up in the air and catching it.)* Okay, so even if Gus can predict storms, what does that have to do with the party?

Jake: I thought we could set up our own weather forecasting service. We can call it Gus's Best Guess.

Michael: So you want to bring Gus to school?

Jake: Yeah, I thought it would be great to have a class pet! We could have a live Guinea Pig Cam in the classroom, so kids can see what he's doing all the time. And we could send out text alerts just like a real weather service!

Tori: It does sound kind of scientific.

Michael: You'd have to ask Mr. Pacella.

Tori: Mr. Pacella is kind of cool. I think he might go for it. But, what about Otto, Jake? Won't he be lonely?

Jake: I don't think Otto will miss him. He and Gus fight all the time. What do you think?

Michael: I don't know, but it might work!

Tori: Would your mom let you bring Gus to school?

Jake: I'll go ask her right now. See you later! *(Jake exits right.)*

(Michael and Tori exit stage left.)

Scene 4: The Classroom – a few weeks later

(Arrange tables and chairs or desks to look like a classroom. Add additional performers to play the parts of other students. Encourage them to act naturally but quietly with other cast members. Several students should be standing at the window.)

Michael: Wow! Everyone's watching the Guinea Pig Cam this morning! That was the best part of our Groundhog Day party, Jake.

Jake: Better than Mr. Pacella in a groundhog costume? 'Cause that was awesome!

Tori: The school TV station is broadcasting Gus's forecasts, and we have more than 500 people subscribing to our text alerts.

Jake: That's because Gus has been right 100% of the time for the last thirty days. That's better than the National Weather Service!

Michael: Channel 2 is only predicting flurries today.

Tori: *(Walking to the window.)* It's snowing really hard. It doesn't look like flurries to me.

Jake: *(Looking in Gus's cage.)* That must be what Gus is trying to tell us.

Michael: Whoa! He pulled most of his cedar chips into his box, too.

Jake: He hasn't come out all morning. He didn't even eat breakfast. I'm really worried.

Michael: Maybe he's sick.

Tori: My mom said there's a big storm coming up the coast, but it's supposed to miss us. Do you think Gus knows something about it?

Jake: Send out a text alert! "Big snowstorm headed this way!"

Michael: What if Gus is wrong?

Jake: What if he isn't? We'll all be stuck at school! The buses won't be able to pick us up! What if the cafeteria runs out of food?

Tori: Or we run out of toilet paper!

Michael: *(Turning to look at her.)* Seriously? You're worried about toilet paper?

Tori: *(Nodding.)* Well, it *is* pretty important.

Michael: Jake, if you're sure about this, I'll send the text.

Tori and **Jake:** Do it!

Mr. Pacella: *(Enters stage right.)* What's up, guys? I got your text. Where's Gus?

Jake: He hasn't come out all morning, and he won't eat.

Mr. Pacella: I hate to ask, but he's not . . . ?

Jake: Dead? No, I can hear him breathing really hard.

Mr. Pacella: So, you're predicting a big storm?

Jake: Gus has been right all month. We've had five snowstorms, and he warned us every time.

Mr. Pacella: Well, he *is* the official school weather mascot. Maybe I'll call the principal. *(He moves to the edge of stage right.)* Class, be quiet while I'm on the phone!

Class: Yes, Mr. Pacella!

Jake: *(In a stage whisper.)* I don't want to go home early.

Tori: Why? Snow days are the best!

Jake: Because I have to finish my project for Mr. Pacella. Monday is the end of the grading period.

Tori: Can you do it at home?

Jake: No, I have to do it here. Shh! He's coming back.

Mr. Pacella: *(Walking back toward the class.)* Well, I guess the principal has faith in guinea pigs. He's decided on an early dismissal. He's calling the bus company now.

Tori: All because of Gus?

Mr. Pacella: Not entirely. The snow is coming down pretty hard. It's better to be safe than sorry. Get your things together, class. The buses will be here shortly.

Jake: What about my special project, Mr. Pacella?

Mr. Pacella: *(Walking away.)* Don't worry about that now, Jake. *(Turning back around.)* And remember, this is Friday. Be sure to take Gus home, too. There won't be anyone to feed him over the weekend.

Scene 5: The Classroom – four days later

(Set the stage the same as for scene 4. Students enter with coats on and begin to take them off.)

Michael: I still can't believe it! The worst storm in twenty years, and a guinea pig called it!

Tori: We had twenty inches of snow at my house!

Michael: We did, too. My mom said if we hadn't been dismissed early on Friday, we would have been stuck at school for three days!

(Jake enters and everyone claps. He makes a silly bow and walks over to Michael and Tori.)

Michael: Way to go, Jake! Gus is a great weather forecaster!

Jake: *(Looking at the floor.)* I need to talk to you guys about a couple of things.

Tori: What's the matter?

Jake: Well first, the grading period is over. I'm going to fail science. And . . .

Mr. Pacella: *(Walks in and everyone gets quiet.)* Well, class, I hope you all had a great snow day! I want to thank Jake and Gus for getting everyone home safely in time.

(Class claps.)

Mr. Pacella: And Jake, for setting up your excellent Gus's Best Guess weather forecasting service, I think we can call your special project complete.

(Class claps.)

Tori: *(Patting Jake on the arm.)* That's great, Jake!

Michael: *(Gives him a high five.)* Way to go!

Mr. Pacella: Where's Gus? I have a little surprise for him, too.

Jake: *(Hesitating.)* Gus is at home, Mr. Pacella. He's . . . ah . . . resting up.

Mr. Pacella: Well, give him these carrots and tell him I want him back on the job!

Jake: I will, sir. Thank you!

Mr. Pacella: Okay, we need to catch up. Open your science books to page 172.

Michael: *(Whispering.)* So, what's the matter? Is there something wrong with Gus? He didn't croak, did he?

Jake: *(Shakes his head.)* That's what I was going to tell you. Gus isn't Gus. He's Gussy.

Tori: What?

Jake: My guinea pig had four babies Friday afternoon. That's why she wouldn't come out of the box.

Michael: No way!

Tori: You're going to have to tell Mr. Pacella.

Jake: I will, but not today. Let's wait until the grades are posted. I've never done this well in science before!

The End

Adapting Readers' Theater Scripts

Readers' theater can be done very simply. Performers just read their lines from scripts. They don't have to memorize them! And, they don't have to move around. The performers sit on chairs or stools while reading their parts.

Adapted Readers' Theater: This looks more like a regular play. The performers wear makeup and costumes. The stage has scenery and props. The cast moves around to show the action. Performers can still read from their scripts.

A Puppet Show: Some schools and libraries have puppet collections. Or students can create puppets. Students make the puppets be the actors. They read their scripts for their puppets.

Teaching Guides

Readers' Theater Teaching Guides are available online at **abdopublishing.com**. Each guide includes printable scripts, reading levels for each character, and additional production tips for each play. Get yours today!

Websites

To learn more about Readers' Theater, visit **booklinks.abdopublishing.com**. These links are routinely monitored and updated to provide the most current information available.